1983
The Year You Were Born

Birth Certificate

Name: ______________________

Birthdate: ______________________

Time: ______________________

Place of Birth: ______________________

Weight: ____________ Length: ________

Mother's maiden name: ______________

Father's name: ______________________

To Christopher and Scott Graham from Auntie Jeanne J.M.

To my sister Carolyn, with love J.L.

 Inquiries should be addressed to
Tambourine Books, a division of William Morrow & Company, Inc.,
1350 Avenue of the Americas, New York, New York 10019.
Printed in the United States of America

Library of Congress Cataloging in Publication Data
Martinet, Jeanne (Jeanne M.)
The year you were born, 1983/by Jeanne Martinet;
illustrated by Judy Lanfredi.—1st ed.
p. cm.
Summary: Presents an assortment of events, news items,
and facts for each day of the year 1983.
ISBN 0-688-11077-0 (T).—ISBN 0-688-11078-9 (L)
1. Nineteen eighty-three, A.D.—Chronology—Juvenile literature.
2. United States—History—1969- —Chronology—Juvenile literature.
[1. Calendars. 2. Nineteen eighty-three, A.D.—Chronology.]
I. Lanfredi, Judy, ill. II. Title.
E876.M363 1992 973.927—dc20 91-31605 CIP AC r91

1 3 5 7 9 10 8 6 4 2
First Edition

1983
The Year You Were Born

Compiled by

JEANNE MARTINET

Illustrated by

JUDY LANFREDI

Tambourine Books New York

U.S. Almanac
1983

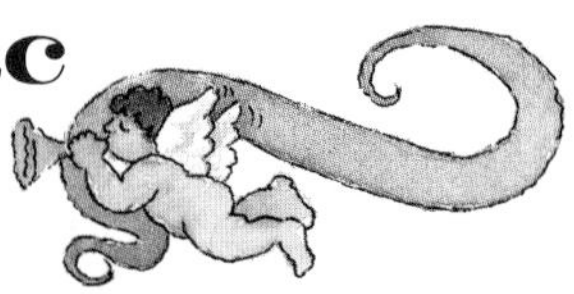

Bicentennial of Air and Space Flight

World Communications Year

World population
4.7 billion

United States population
234,799,000

Size of U.S.
3,618,770 square miles

Persons per square mile 65 (approximation)

President
Ronald Reagan

Largest city
New York, population 7,071,639

Biggest state (in area)
Alaska, 591,004 square miles

Number of births in U.S.
3,639,000
Boys 1,866,000
Girls 1,773,000

Average length at birth 1 foot, 8 inches
Average weight at birth 7½ pounds

Deaths in U.S.
2,019,000

People 100 years old or older in the U.S.
32,000

Tornadoes
931

Households with television sets
83,300,000
Households with VCRs
4,580,000

Average television-viewing time for Americans ages 6–11
24 hours per week

Top crop
Corn
Total 1983 output
106 million metric tons

Children's books sold
205,000,000

Top movie (highest earnings)
Return of the Jedi, $232.3 million

Top spectator sport
Baseball, which drew 78,061,343 fans

Patent applications (new inventions)
105,704

Most popular girl's name
Jennifer
Most popular boy's name
Michael

Most rain
Miami, Florida, 67.41 inches
Most snow
Caribou, Maine, 135.7 inches

January

*J*anuary is named after Janus, the Roman god of doorways and of beginnings.

BIRTHSTONE *Garnet*

SATURDAY
January 1

New Year's Day • In college football games, Penn State beats Georgia in the Sugar Bowl in New Orleans 27–23. At the Rose Bowl in Pasadena, California, the University of California at Los Angeles beats Michigan 24–14.

SUNDAY
January 2

The freighter *Cariari* sinks in Biscayne Bay, Florida, carrying 2,000 tons of frozen meat.

MONDAY
January 3

President Ronald Reagan issues a proclamation declaring 1983 to be the Bicentennial of Air and Space Flight. • Kilauea, a volcano in Hawaii, erupts.

TUESDAY
January 4

BUNGLING BURGLAR: In Charlotte, North Carolina, an intruder breaks into a doctor's office and, rather than steal anything, leaves a note saying, "Sorry. Wrong building, Doc."

WEDNESDAY
January 5

In San Diego, California, Rusty and Jamie, two of the first pelicans ever to be fitted with artificial beaks (after vandals sawed the real ones off), are shipped to Sea World on their way back to the wild.

THURSDAY
January 6

Pope John Paul II names 18 new cardinals. • In Burlington, Iowa, officials begin dismantling a car that they found had somehow gotten into the sewers!

FRIDAY
January 7

American astronomers in the Andes in Chile have discovered a new black hole in space, just beyond the Milky Way. • The Great American Motorcycle Show opens in Fort Worth, Texas. • Strong earthquakes rock central California.

SATURDAY
January 8

NOISY NEIGHBORS: 500,000 chirping starlings have moved into a grove of cedar trees in Washington, Missouri. Even firecrackers won't scare them away.

WHO ELSE WAS BORN IN JANUARY?

MARTIN LUTHER KING, Jr.

U.S. civil rights leader
Began nonviolent crusade for black rights with boycott of buses in Montgomery, Alabama, in 1955; received the Nobel Peace Prize in 1964 for his work on behalf of racial equality in the U.S.
BORN January 15, 1929, in Atlanta, Georgia

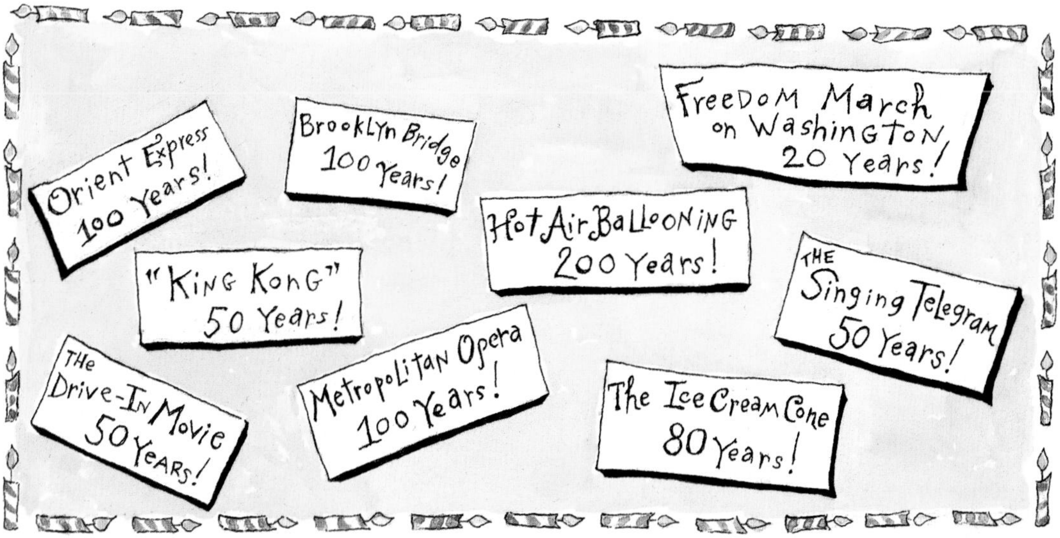
Orient Express 100 Years!
Brooklyn Bridge 100 Years!
Freedom March on Washington 20 Years!
Hot Air Ballooning 200 Years!
"King Kong" 50 Years!
The Singing Telegram 50 Years!
The Drive-In Movie 50 Years!
Metropolitan Opera 100 Years!
The Ice Cream Cone 80 Years!

SUNDAY *January 9* — Archaeologists remove part of a skeleton near Austin, Texas. It's been buried for almost 9,000 years!

MONDAY *January 10* — The town of Belle Glade, Florida, announces its plans to build the world's biggest salad, using the local crop of lettuce, celery, and radishes.

TUESDAY *January 11* — The governor of Georgia, George Busbee, leaves office today. He has, however, been offered the job of dogcatcher!

WEDNESDAY *January 12* — Officials in San Joaquin County, California, are putting a Pac-Man machine and other video games in the jury room to make waiting to serve as a juror more enjoyable.

THURSDAY
January 13

Five hundred people—and about 6,000 pigeons!—attend the Grand National Fancy Pigeon Show in Lincoln, Nebraska.

FRIDAY
January 14

The American Medical Association has urged a ban on boxing because of its effects on boxers' health and physical condition.

SATURDAY
January 15

Today is Martin Luther King, Jr.'s birthday. He was born in 1929.

SUNDAY
January 16

National Nothing Day, first observed in 1973. • In Cheektowaga, New York, Joe Carson has close to a million points (a world record) in the Defender video game he has been playing for more than three days.

MONDAY
January 17

George Wallace becomes the first man to be inaugurated for a fourth term as governor of Alabama.

TUESDAY
January 18

Demonstrators carry 30-foot-long whale balloons outside the White House to protest Japan's refusal to end commercial whaling.

WEDNESDAY
January 19

A Chicago foundation, the John D. and Catherine T. MacArthur foundation, has selected 18 men and 2 women to receive between $24,000 and $60,000 a year for life, just for being exceptionally talented!

THURSDAY
January 20

A robber in Warren, Ohio, gets a big surprise when the barrel of his gun falls off as he aims it at a salesclerk.

FRIDAY
January 21

Scientists at the University of Chicago have started building the world's most powerful microscope, which will be able to magnify objects 150 million times and will make it possible to see individual atoms.

SATURDAY
January 22

PARACHUTING PIGS: Dressed in goggles and scarves, three pigs—Ralph, Betty, and Mabel—are strapped to the backs of skydivers for the Great American Pig-Out, an outdoor music festival in St. Petersburg, Florida. Unfortunately, low clouds force them to cancel the pig jump!

SUNDAY
January 23

National Handwriting Day, which is observed on John Hancock's birthday and encourages more legible handwriting.

MONDAY
January 24

Earthquakes hit southeastern Mexico and the Andaman Islands in the Bay of Bengal in Southeast Asia.

TUESDAY
January 25

IRAS, the most powerful infrared telescope ever made, is launched into orbit from the Vandenberg Air Force Base in California. Its mission: to scan the galaxy for signs of stars, asteroids, and planets.

FUN FACT '83

January 1983 marks the 14th consecutive year in which 69-year-old Arthur Holmson has managed to get into Disneyland free!

WEDNESDAY
January 26

After a forty-year search, Swiss physicists have finally discovered the subatomic W particle.

THURSDAY
January 27

The hole for the longest railroad tunnel in the world (33.46 miles) is completed today in Japan.

FRIDAY
January 28
Full Moon

A police dog, a German shepherd named Gator, gets a new silver fang in Oklahoma. • In Texas, a sandhill crane named Bonaparte has artificial legs put on, made from plastic pipes and suction cups.

SATURDAY
January 29

Secretary of State George Shultz leaves on a 12-day mission to the Far East to try to smooth out problems that have arisen in Chinese-American relations.

SUNDAY
January 30

The Washington Redskins beat the Miami Dolphins in the Super Bowl as 40,480,000 households watch on television. • Twiggy, the water-skiing squirrel, performs at the boat show in Minneapolis.

MONDAY
January 31

The longest teachers' strike in Pennsylvania's history ends after 82 days. Back to class!

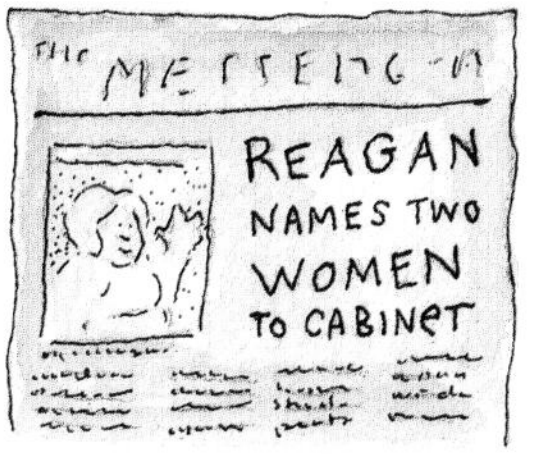

February

*T*he name February comes from the Latin *Februa*, which means "feast of purification."

BIRTHSTONE *Amethyst*

TUESDAY
February 1

Tina, a 25-year-old, 9,000-pound Central Park Zoo elephant who has had trouble finding a home because of her bad temper, boards a truck in New York City bound for Redwood City, California.

WEDNESDAY
February 2

Groundhog Day • A record 16 tornadoes sweep across Florida, and there is flooding in Alabama and North Carolina.

THURSDAY
February 3

In Washington, Mount St. Helens spurts mud down its slopes and sprays ash for 100 miles around in two small explosions, the first signs of activity from the volcano in more than five months.

FRIDAY
February 4

Billy Olson of the Pacific Coast Club sets the U.S. indoor record in field with a 19-foot, $3/8$-inch pole vault at the Toronto Star Maple Leaf Games.

SATURDAY
February 5

Snow has been diverted from Moscow this winter by aircraft dropping dry ice into clouds approaching the city. This brings the snow down sooner!

SUNDAY
February 6

An 80-pound mechanical ape, who usually waves at passengers driving by, is stolen from its service-station home in Collinsville, Illinois.

MONDAY
February 7

Tina, the elephant with the grumpy disposition, arrives at her new home in Marine World–Africa USA, Redwood City, California. She is greeted by a new elephant friend, Margie.

TUESDAY
February 8

Anniversary of the founding of the Boy Scouts of America • The famous racehorse Shergar, valued at $13.5 million, is kidnapped by gunmen from its farm in County Kildare, Ireland.

WEDNESDAY
February 9

The chancellor of New York City's schools announces a new policy requiring that all pupils be assigned a certain amount of homework every night.

THURSDAY
February 10

The U.S. Postal Service issues an Olympic commemorative coin. The profits from its sale will help fund the training of amateur athletes.

FRIDAY
February 11

National Inventors Day • The 80th annual American Toy Fair takes place in New York City. • Albert McReynolds receives $250,000 for catching a 78½-pound striped bass, the largest ever caught.

SATURDAY
February 12

Lincoln's birthday • The East Coast is paralyzed by a record-breaking blizzard, with up to 35 inches of snow in some areas. • The coal freighter *Marine Electric* sinks in waters off Chincoteague, Virginia.

SUNDAY
February 13

Beginning of the Chinese Year of the Pig • At the International Strange Music Weekend in Olive Hill, Kentucky, the Savannah Sheiks sing a song called "Booglie-Wooglie Piggy-Wiggy with the Oink, Oink."

MONDAY
February 14

Valentine's Day • Giant wooden hearts are hung from street lamps in Loveland, Colorado, which calls itself "Sweetheart City."

TUESDAY
February 15

An Eastern Airline 727 comes down safely on its belly in Miami, Florida, after the discovery that there is something wrong with the landing gear.

SOME INVENTIONS OF 1983

February 11 is National Inventors Day

- The vacuum-cleaning robot
- The aromatic disk player (emits smells instead of music)
- The graphite-fiber violin
- The cordless telephone
- The talking camera
- The nursing robot
- Rubik's Snake
- The pomato
- ZooDoo
- Tubble gum
- The TV wristwatch

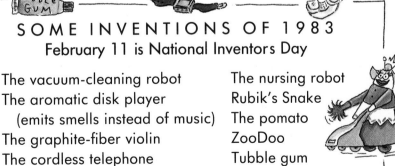

WHO ELSE WAS BORN IN FEBRUARY?

ABRAHAM LINCOLN

Lawyer, politician, 16th U.S. President
He led the Union through the Civil War.
BORN February 12, 1809, in Hardin County, Kentucky

WEDNESDAY *February 16* Ash Wednesday • St. Albans, Vermont, announces plans to build the biggest ice-cream sundae in the world.

THURSDAY *February 17* ANTIQUE AMMUNITION: Construction crews dig up 50 live Civil War cannonballs in a parking lot in Houston, Texas.

FRIDAY *February 18* 38-year-old baseball pitcher Tom Seaver, who has not played with the New York Mets for six years, injures his leg today—the first day of spring training!

SATURDAY *February 19* International Skate-a-thon on Lake Memphremagog, between Newport, Vermont, and Magog, Quebec, Canada.

SUNDAY *February 20* A baby tarsier (a small primate with large round eyes and a long tail) is born at the Stockholm Zoo in Sweden. He is named E.T.!

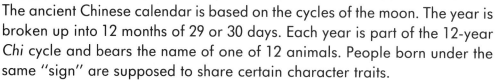

1983: CHINESE YEAR OF THE PIG

February 13, 1983–February 1, 1984

The ancient Chinese calendar is based on the cycles of the moon. The year is broken up into 12 months of 29 or 30 days. Each year is part of the 12-year *Chi* cycle and bears the name of one of 12 animals. People born under the same "sign" are supposed to share certain character traits.

Pigs are gallant, trustworthy, truthful, and confident! They are also good sports, good workers, and good at making money. Pigs go well with Hares but not with Snakes or Sheep. Famous Pigs include Henry Ford, Richard Dreyfuss, Ronald Reagan, Marcel Marceau, Tennessee Williams, Harry Reasoner, William Randolph Hearst, Vincent Price, and Henry Kissinger.

The 12-year cycle: 1983—Pig; 1984—Rat; 1985—Ox; 1986—Tiger; 1987—Hare; 1988—Dragon; 1989—Snake; 1990—Horse; 1991—Sheep; 1992—Monkey; 1993—Rooster; 1994—Dog.

The Chinese New Year's celebration, called *Hsin Nien*, begins at the first new moon after the sun enters Aquarius. It lasts four days!

MONDAY
February 21

Scientists at Kansas State University have figured out how to cross a tomato with a potato. The result: the "pomato," a small yellow fruit.

TUESDAY
February 22

George Washington's birthday • The U.S. Supreme Court rules that the makers of the board game Monopoly no longer have a monopoly on the game's name.

FUN FACT '83

Abraham Lincoln didn't always have his famous beard; he grew it after an 11-year-old girl told him it would make his face look better.

WEDNESDAY
February 23

Television viewers in Phoenix, Arizona, watch open-heart surgery, live from the operating room!

THURSDAY
February 24

Rocket controllers are forced to destroy an unarmed missile after it develops problems on its test flight to the Marshall Islands.

FRIDAY
February 25

Cattle Show and Sale in Houston. Fifty longhorn cattle parade across the stage while diners in tuxedos and gowns look on.

SATURDAY
February 26

Queen Elizabeth and Prince Philip arrive in San Diego on their royal yacht for a ten-day visit to the United States and Canada. It's the queen's first trip to America since 1976.

SUNDAY
February 27
Full Moon

J. R. Ingel wins the chicken-hypnotizing contest in Apache, Oklahoma.

MONDAY
February 28

The last episode of the popular television program *M.A.S.H.* is aired on CBS to approximately 121,624,000 viewers.

PRIZE RACE HORSE SHERGAR KIDNAPPED IN IRELAND

SNOWSTORM PARALYZES MID-ATLANTIC U.S.

EX-GESTAPO LEADER RETURNED TO FRANCE

QUEEN ELIZABETH TOURS U.S. WEST COAST

March

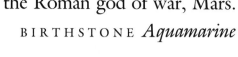

*M*arch is named for the Roman god of war, Mars.

BIRTHSTONE *Aquamarine*

TUESDAY
March 1
Queen Elizabeth and Prince Philip visit President and Mrs. Reagan at their California ranch in the midst of severe storms, including a tornado.

WEDNESDAY
March 2
A fire in a manhole cuts off electric power to Boston's downtown financial district at the height of evening rush hour, throwing the heart of the city into darkess for nearly a day.

THURSDAY
March 3
Dolls' Day in Japan • In Denver, Colorado, an awed crowd watches as 8,000 dominoes are toppled and 1,000 balloons sent up to publicize the opening of a new shopping mall.

FRIDAY
March 4
U.S. Constitution Day, the anniversary of the meeting of the first Congress in New York City in 1789 • In Stamford, Connecticut, the American Crossword Puzzle Tournament begins.

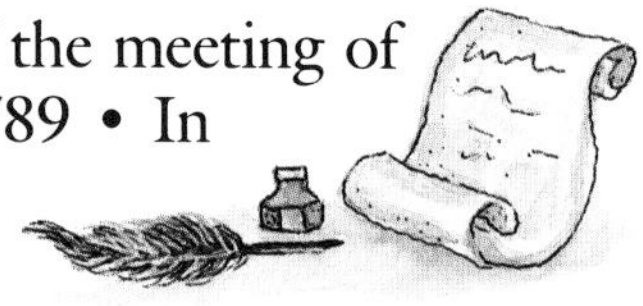

SATURDAY
March 5
A brand-new, 17,000-gallon water tower in Bayside, Texas, splits and then collapses as it is being filled for the first time. • In nearby Hermleigh, Texas, a pig is sold for the amazing sum of $56,000!

SUNDAY
March 6

A cross-country skier in Utah is buried in an avalanche but is rescued 20 minutes later because of a radio transmitter he is wearing.

MONDAY
March 7
A newly purchased 700-pound cow named Julieann leaps over two 4-foot barbed-wire fences and travels 35 miles to get back to her home in Geneva, Florida.

COSTLY CONDORS

The California condor is actually a species of vulture (*Gymnogyps californianus*) and is facing extinction. The cost of raising the rare California condors that live at the San Diego Zoo is about $200,000 a year—including $40,000 for mice they eat. Each of the chicks dines on up to 300 mice a day!

TUESDAY
March 8

A group of second-graders from Montana lobby their state representative for a four-day school week, 30-minute recess, and no enchiladas on the lunch menu.

U.S. EARTHQUAKES OF 1983

An earthquake occurs when there is a deep fracture, or fault, in the earth's rocky crust. Over many years, the edges of the fault bump and grind against each other without our noticing it. A sideways movement is called a strike-slip fault; an up-and-down movement is called a dip-slip fault. Sometimes, however, there are upheavals that can be felt for miles and that cause considerable damage.

January 7	Central California	August 24	Northwest California
May 2	Central California	October 8	New York State
May 15	St. Louis, Missouri, and southwest Illinois	October 28	Northwestern U.S. (8 states)
June 10	Central California	November 15	Hawaii

Many people say the safest place to stand during an earthquake is in a doorway!

WEDNESDAY
March 9

President Reagan declares video games to be good for the nation.

THURSDAY
March 10

It's Mario Day in Chicago! If your name is Mario, you're invited to the annual MarioFest.

FRIDAY
March 11

Bloomingdale, Illinois, celebrates its 150th birthday. To honor the occasion, starting today, any man in town who does not have a mustache will be fined $1.98.

SATURDAY
March 12

Anniversary of the founding of the American Girl Scouts in 1912 by Juliette Gordon Low.

SUNDAY
March 13

A poisonous frog, some snakes, and a tarantula are stolen from a store in Los Angeles. The frog is mysteriously back in its cage the next day!

MONDAY
March 14

MISSING: Bird specialists report that the 16.5 million birds that usually inhabit Christmas Island in the Pacific have disappeared.

TUESDAY
March 15

People in Hinkley, Ohio, scan the skies for the season's first buzzards. For the last 150 years, between 75 and 100 of the big birds have returned to the town on the Ides of March. First sighting today: 8:21 A.M.

WEDNESDAY
March 16

NASA scientists have concluded that a rock found in Antarctica four years ago is actually from the moon, making it the first moon rock found on Earth.

THURSDAY
March 17

St. Patrick's Day • In Dublin, Ireland, a giant model of E.T. reigns over the annual St. Paddy's Day Parade.

FRIDAY
March 18

Prehistoric markings at the edge of the Painted Desert in Arizona have been determined by a NASA astronomer to be an ancient solar calendar.

SATURDAY
March 19

Swallow Day in California. Since 1776, this has been the traditional date for swallows to return to the old mission of San Juan Capistrano.

SUNDAY
March 20

Spring equinox • About 40,000 people turn out for the homecoming party for the buzzards of Hinkley, Ohio.

FUN FACT '83

Every dog in the world has its own unique nose print.

MONDAY
March 21

Governor Robert D. Orr of Indiana and a cow named Betsy win the Agriculture Day milking contest in Indianapolis.

TUESDAY
March 22

National Goof-Off Day • In New York City, ZooDoo—a fertilizer made from the droppings of hippos, rhinos, elephants, kangaroos, giraffes, and zebras from the Bronx Zoo—is introduced to the public at a news conference.

WEDNESDAY
March 23

President Reagan proposes the development of a new technology for intercepting incoming enemy missiles, which later becomes known as "Star Wars."

HI-TECH REST

In 1983, some of the animals at the San Diego Zoo are sleeping on water beds! The beds are heated, which keeps the animal warm, and even tigers can't claw through the flexible aluminum with which they are made.

WHO ELSE WAS BORN IN MARCH?

DARYL STRAWBERRY

Baseball player; outfielder
In 1983, he was named Rookie of the Year.
BORN March 12, 1962, in Los Angeles, California

THURSDAY
March 24
The first American test-tube twins are born at 10:53 and 10:54 A.M. on Long Island in New York. • Residents in three New York–area counties spot boomerang-shaped UFOs in the night sky.

FRIDAY
March 25
The U.S. Postal Service adds a 3-cent stamp to its ongoing transportation series. This one pictures an antique, two-man handcar.

SATURDAY
March 26
The Smithsonian Institution holds its 17th annual kite festival in Washington, D.C.

SUNDAY
March 27
Palm Sunday • Antique bottle show in Kentucky, is sponsored by the Antique Bottle and Outhouse Society.

MONDAY
March 28
Full Moon
Officials at the Randolph, Massachusetts, post office discover that stamps worth more than $100,000 have been stolen.

TUESDAY
March 29
First day of Passover • The American water spaniel becomes Wisconsin's official dog.

WEDNESDAY
March 30
The first California condor chick born in captivity hatches at the San Diego Zoo. It is named Sisquoc.

THURSDAY
March 31
Major earthquake in southern Colombia. • The U.S. Postal Service issues a new block of four stamps today, heralding hot-air ballooning.

GIANT PANDAS MATE
AT WASHINGTON ZOO

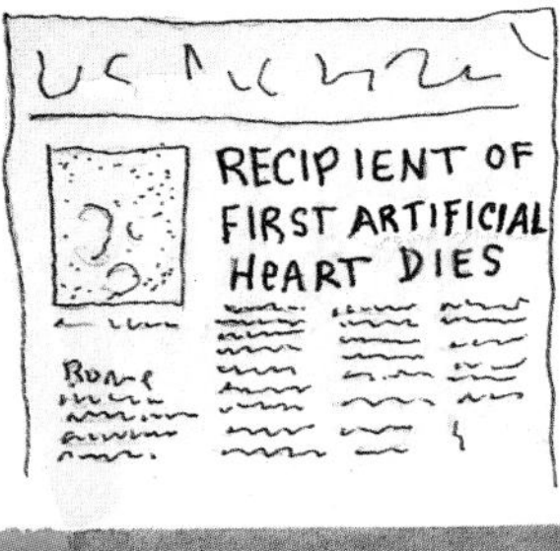
RECIPIENT OF
FIRST ARTIFICIAL
HEART DIES

MAJOR EARTHQUAKE
IN COLUMBIA

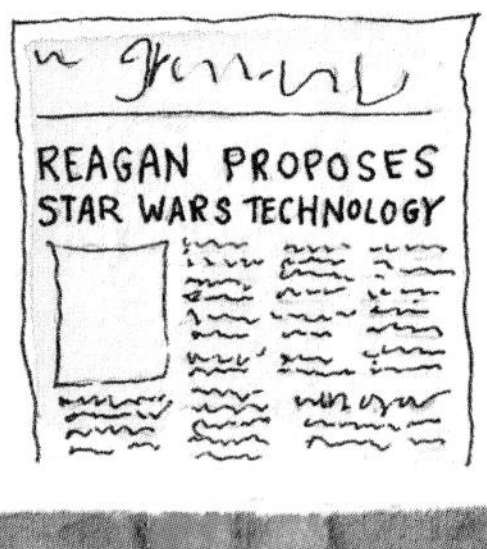
REAGAN PROPOSES
STAR WARS TECHNOLOGY

April

*T*he name April comes from the Latin *aperire*, which means "to open." April is known as the time of budding.

BIRTHSTONE *Diamond*

FRIDAY
April 1

April Fools' Day • Utah, usually the nation's second-driest state, suffers severe rainstorms, causing the Great Salt Lake to rise to its highest level since the 1920s.

SATURDAY
April 2

A large, flaming white fireball streaks across southern California at night, disappearing over the Pacific Ocean. Officials believe it is an object from outer space!

SUNDAY
April 3

Easter • The world's largest Easter egg hunt—30,000 eggs —is held at Stone Mountain Park outside Atlanta.

MONDAY
April 4

The U.S. grants political asylum to Hu Na, China's leading woman tennis player.

TUESDAY
April 5

Blizzard paralyzes western U.S. • A 16-year-old boy is bitten by one of the two five-foot-long gaboon vipers he has stolen from the National Zoo in Washington, D.C.

WEDNESDAY
April 6

An 84-foot-high gorilla balloon is being put up on top of the Empire State Building for the 50th anniversary of the movie *King Kong*. • Today is also the anniversary of Robert Peary's discovery of the North Pole in 1909.

THURSDAY
April 7

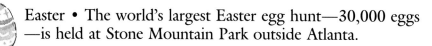

Two astronauts from the shuttle *Challenger*, in the first space walk in nine years, glide and tumble outside the craft for almost four hours.

FRIDAY
April 8

Happy birthday to the founder of Buddhism, Gautama Buddha! • Nearly 20 inches of rain in Louisiana, Mississippi, and Alabama has forced thousands to evacuate their homes in one of the most disastrous floods in history.

SATURDAY
April 9

The space shuttle *Challenger* lands, having completed its five-day mission. • In Valhalla, New York, a small plane runs out of gas and makes an emergency landing on a state highway.

SUNDAY
April 10

Gross National Parade in Washington, D.C., the city's first annual tribute to silliness. • In Long Beach, California, a group sings "Yellow Submarine" underwater to raise money for the Handicapped Scuba Association.

MONDAY
April 11

A healthy, twin-humped, 80-pound Bactrian camel is born at the St. Louis Zoo. Only about 200 of these camels exist in the wild.

TUESDAY
April 12

Chicago elects its first black mayor, Harold Washington. • The movie *E.T.: The Extraterrestrial*, after breaking all box-office records, has just won four Oscars!

WEDNESDAY
April 13

After three attempts and a rip in the gorilla's shoulder, the King Kong balloon is finally successfully inflated on top of the Empire State Building.

THURSDAY
April 14

The first cordless telephone is put on the market today.

FRIDAY
April 15

MICKEY GOES JAPANESE: Tokyo Disneyland opens, the first Disneyland park outside the U.S. It cost $600 million to build.

CONDOR UPDATE

A second California condor chick hatches at the San Diego Zoo on April 5, six days after the first. This one is named Tecuya!

SATURDAY
April 16

The 2.74 inches of rain today in New York City makes April 1983 the wettest April (10.04 inches so far) since 1874. • Dumb Songs Festival in San Francisco; National Whistlers Convention in Louisburg, North Carolina.

SUNDAY
April 17

IF ONLY THEY COULD TALK: Museum officials report that they are still searching for George Washington's false teeth, which disappeared from the National Museum of American History in June 1981. The uppers were returned (anonymously) in May 1982.

MONDAY
April 18

The 87th Boston Marathon is won by Greg Meyer of Wellesley, Massachusetts, in 2 hours, 9 minutes. • Joan Benoit wins women's division in world record time of 2 hours, 22 minutes, 42 seconds.

WHO ELSE WAS BORN IN APRIL?

LEONARDO DA VINCI

Italian painter, sculptor, architect, musician, and scientist The ultimate Renaissance man, he is considered to be one of the world's greatest geniuses.
BORN April 15, 1452, in Italy

TUESDAY
April 19
Los Angeles International Airport employees chase escaped cattle off two of the runways and finally corral them in the baggage area!

WEDNESDAY
April 20
Controlled by police using remote control, a bomb-removal robot carries a suspicious-looking briefcase to a special disposal truck. It turns out the case contains only tools.

THURSDAY
April 21
Happy birthday to the queen of England • A late freeze has devastated fruit and vegetables from the Carolinas to Arkansas.

FUN FACT '83

In Washington, D.C., there are 1,730 telephones for every 1,000 people!

FRIDAY
April 22
Arbor Day • West Germany announces the discovery of what it believes to be 60 volumes of diaries by Adolph Hitler, which a journalist found in a hayloft.

SATURDAY
April 23
It's Peppercorn Day in Bermuda. • In Benton, Tennessee, hundreds flock to Big Frog Mountain to eat "ramps"—smelly, onionlike wild vegetables—for the Polk County Ramp Tramp.

LETTER TO E.T.?

On April 25, the U.S. space probe *Pioneer 10* zooms past Pluto, traveling farther than any object previously sent by humans. Its purpose: to contact alien civilizations. Launched in 1972, the probe is aimed at a point in space between the constellations Taurus and Orion; it will take *Pioneer 10* more than 100,000 years to get near the stars in that area! If any beings ever do receive our "message," what they will find is a series of scientific symbols, a map of our Solar System's nine planets, and pictures of two naked human beings (male and female). On June 13, 1983, *Pioneer 10* will become the first man-made object to leave the Solar System.

SUNDAY
April 24

DAYLIGHT SAVINGS VERSUS EASTERN STANDARD: Union City, Ohio, which is right on the border between time zones, goes through its usual confusion when half the residents put their clocks ahead an hour and the other half don't.

MONDAY
April 25

The U.S. space probe *Pioneer 10*, launched in 1972, zooms past Pluto today. It is the first man-made object to travel such a distance from Earth.

TUESDAY
April 26

Eight explorers from an Ohio spelunking club are rescued from a cavern in Mount Vernon, Kentucky, after being trapped inside by high water for three days.

VACUUM, PHONE HOME

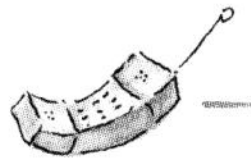

A doctor in California has no idea he is racking up a hefty phone bill. Without his knowledge, his vacuum cleaner is electronically dialing strange numbers on his cordless phone. . . .

WEDNESDAY
April 27
Full Moon

Ten-year-old Carol Guthrie wins the spelling bee in the Chattanooga–Hamilton County finals. She will go on to compete in the national bee in Washington, D.C.

THURSDAY
April 28

Aircraft carrier *Enterprise* runs aground in the mud in San Francisco Bay only half a mile from where it is supposed to dock.

FRIDAY
April 29

The New Orleans Jazz and Heritage Festival begins. • More than 400 doctors in Atlanta announce the formation of a nonprofit corporation that will provide free medical treatment to the jobless.

SATURDAY
April 30

A flock of hundreds of Vaux's swifts swoops down the chimney of the Melton family in Santa Paula, California. It's the second time in a week that the birds have invaded the Meltons' home!

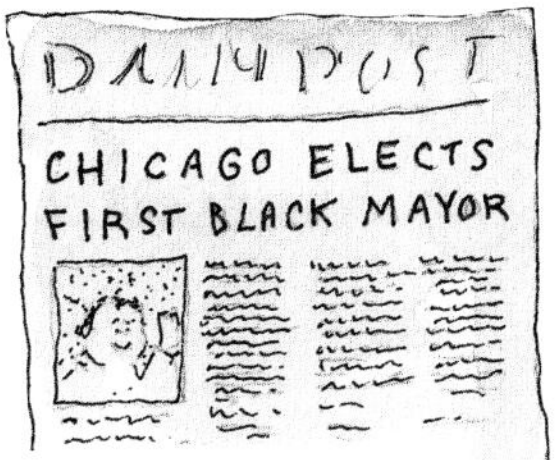
CHICAGO ELECTS FIRST BLACK MAYOR

U.S. GRANTS ASYLUM TO CHINESE TENNIS PLAYER

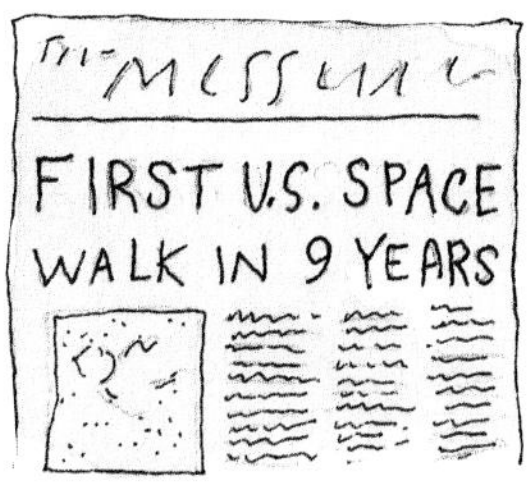
FIRST U.S. SPACE WALK IN 9 YEARS

BOMB EXPLODES AT U.S. EMBASSY IN BEIRUT

May

*M*ay comes from Maia, who was the Roman goddess of growth, increase, and blossoming.

BIRTHSTONE *Emerald*

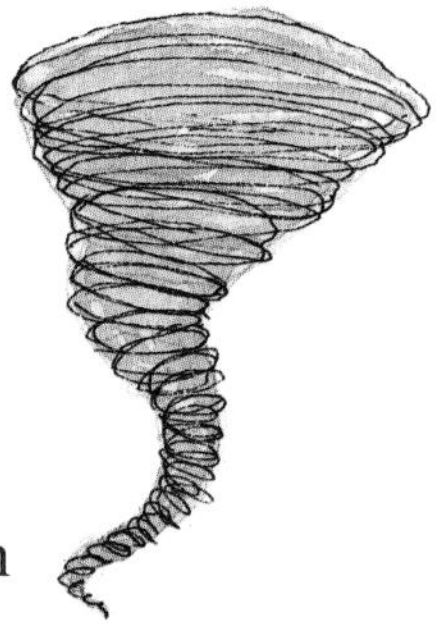

SUNDAY *May 1* — May Day • More than two dozen tornadoes hit the Midwest. • An airplane traveling from Puerto Rico to Miami is hijacked to Cuba.

MONDAY *May 2* — Central California is struck by the strongest earthquake to hit the state in 12 years! Downtown Coalinga is leveled.

TUESDAY *May 3* — Police in Cherry Hill, New Jersey, spend the day chasing an 800-pound black-and-white bull that has gone on a rampage through the suburban town.

WEDNESDAY *May 4* — The artist Christo and his crew begin unfolding 6.5 million square feet of pink plastic which will be wrapped around each of 11 tiny islands in Biscayne Bay, Florida, for a spectacular project called *Surrounded Islands.* The plastic will extend 200 feet out from each island.

THURSDAY *May 5* — DOES MONEY GROW ON TREES? A U.S. geological survey reported that there are traces of gold in some of the trees in Idaho.

FRIDAY *May 6* — The much-talked-about Hitler diaries, found earlier this year in Germany, are proven to be forgeries.

SATURDAY *May 7* — Sunny's Halo wins the Kentucky Derby. • Christo's pink plastic art project in Florida is completed today.

SUNDAY *May 8* — Mother's Day • Also World Red Cross Day • Yugoslavia wins the men's doubles World Table Tennis Championship in Tokyo.

MONDAY
May 9

At 7:11 A.M., in the 56-foot black cutter *Credit Agricole*, Philippe Jeantot of France crosses the finish line in Newport, Rhode Island to win the first organized solo boat race around the world. Time: 159 days, 2 hours, 26 minutes. Distance: 27,550 miles.

TUESDAY
May 10

Raymond Colette, a seventh-grader, wins first place in the Central Park sailboat race in New York City.

WEDNESDAY
May 11

Comet IRAS-Araki-Alcock today comes closer to earth (2.9 million miles) than any other known object has since 1770.

THURSDAY
May 12

The world's largest Key lime pie, measuring 7 feet in diameter and made with 1,152 Key limes, is cut and served by Governor Bob Graham of Florida.

FRIDAY
May 13

It's Friday the 13th. • The Milwaukee Zoo received a gorilla named Tino this week from a zoo in West Germany. Just their luck: Tino only understands German!

SATURDAY
May 14

A scientist in Baton Rouge, Louisiana, has discovered how to make medicine from a certain type of alga.

FUN FACT '83

There are more kangaroos than there are people in Australia—about 19 million kangaroos and only 15 million people!

SUNDAY
May 15

Tom Petranoff breaks the world record in Los Angeles with a javelin throw of 327 feet, 2 inches. • Minor earthquake shakes St. Louis and southwest Illinois.

MONDAY
May 16

Schoolchildren in Moscow have collected 50,000 tons of scrap metal for recycling.

TUESDAY
May 17

The U.S.'s first international food trade show starts in Atlanta. • Environmentalists report that the timber rattlesnake is an endangered species.

WEDNESDAY
May 18

A tornado is sweeping through Texas, and there is a snowstorm blustering in Denver, Colorado. • Mount St. Helens is declared a national monument.

THURSDAY
May 19

Another plane—a New York–bound Eastern Airlines flight—is hijacked to Cuba. It's the third such hijacking in 19 days!

FRIDAY
May 20

The space shuttle *Enterprise*, on its way to the Paris Air Show on the back of a Boeing 747, stops in Gloucestershire, England, to refuel.

1983 AWARDS BOARD

Nobel Peace Prize: Lech Walesa
National Teacher of the Year: LeRoy E. Hay
National Junior Fire Marshall Program Gold Medal: Nolan Hughes
National Spelling Bee Champion: Blake Giddens
Best Movie of 1983 (Academy Award):
Terms of Endearment
Best Special Effects (Academy Award):
Return of the Jedi
Grammy Award (album): Michael Jackson, *Thriller*
Grammy Award (single): Michael Jackson, "Beat It"
Male Athlete of the Year: Carl Lewis, track and field
Female Athlete of the Year: Martina Navratilova, tennis
1983 Newbery Medal for Children's Literature: Cynthia Voight, *Dicey's Song*

AWARDS SPOTLIGHT

Carlo Rubia is named Scientist of the Year for his discovery of two elementary particles of matter. His favorite saying? "Physics is fun!"

WHO ELSE WAS BORN IN MAY?

SALLY RIDE

Astronaut, physicist
She became the first U.S. woman in space when the space shuttle *Challenger* was launched on June 18, 1983; she was also the youngest U.S. astronaut in space!
BORN May 26, 1951, in Los Angeles, California

SATURDAY
May 21

Sarah Denu, age 14, sets a flying-trapeze record in Madison, Wisconsin, with 1,350 downward circles otherwise known as "muscle grinders." • The first annual Yoyo-lympics are held in New York City.

SUNDAY
May 22

Citizens of Shepherdstown, West Virginia, honor their local hero, James Rumsey—who they claim is the real inventor of the steamboat—by chugging up the Potomac River in homemade contraptions.

MONDAY
May 23

The famous pirate Captain Kidd was hung on this day in 1701. • Astronomers report they may have located a planet outside our Solar System, 450 light-years from earth!

TUESDAY
May 24

Happy 100th birthday, Brooklyn Bridge! In New York City, more than 2 million jubilant people watch as 9,000 fireworks light up the sky after the day's gala celebration, which included a parade of horse-drawn carriages and marching bands.

WEDNESDAY
May 25

The movie *Return of the Jedi* opens to a record box office of $6,219,929, the highest single-day gross in movie history to date.

THURSDAY
May 26
Full Moon

A tidal wave, caused by a violent earthquake, hits Japan. • 300 helium-filled balloons are launched from a school in West Orange, New Jersey, for a distance/direction experiment. Each one has a postcard with a student's name attached to it.

FRIDAY
May 27

Three dangerous rare crocodiles are missing from a zoo pool in Key Biscayne, Florida. • The balloon that has traveled farthest in yesterday's balloon experiment comes down today—in Chester, Vermont!

SATURDAY
May 28

It's the 14th annual Mule Days weekend in Bishop, California. This year, 335 mules are judged for looks and ability.

SUNDAY
May 29

Tom Sneva wins the Indianapolis 500, with an average speed of 162.117 miles per hour.

MONDAY
May 30

Memorial Day • America's first stand-up roller coaster—the Extremeroller—opens at Worlds of Fun, an amusement park in Kansas City, Missouri.

TUESDAY
May 31

ZOO ART: A footprint of an elephant named Lois is auctioned today at the Kansas City Zoo in Missouri to raise money to enlarge the elephant quarters. Also for sale: finger paintings by chimps, and scratchings made by birds.

WHAT'S NEW IN GEOLOGY? SOMETHING VERY OLD

In May 1983, a team of scientists from the Australian National University in Canberra reports the discovery of the oldest rock ever found. Grains of the rock, which is called zircon, were extracted from sandstone on Mount Narryer in western Australia and are estimated to be between 4.1 billion and 4.2 billion years old! The oldest known rocks before this discovery were found in Greenland in 1971. They were only 3.8 billion years old.

500 DIE WHEN NILE STEAMER SINKS IN CROCODILE INFESTED WATERS

HITLER DIARIES A HOAX

MAJOR QUAKE SHAKES COALINGA CALIFORNIA

NY CELEBRATES 100 TH ANNIVERSARY OF BROOKLYN BRIDGE

June

*J*une is named for the Latin *juniores*, meaning "youths," or from the Roman goddess Juno.

BIRTHSTONE *Pearl*

WEDNESDAY
June 1

Swiss scientists confirm the existence of the Z-zero subnuclear particle.

THURSDAY
June 2

An unmanned Soviet spacecraft, *Venera 15*, is launched; it should go into orbit around Venus in October.

FRIDAY
June 3

The floodlights at the top of the Empire State Building will be turned off this month during any foggy or cloudy weather to keep migrating birds from flying into the building.

SATURDAY
June 4

A passenger ship rams into a railroad bridge on the Volga River in the USSR. • In Jackson, Mississippi, things are sizzling at the 1983 National Farm-raised Catfish Cooking Contest.

SUNDAY
June 5

Today is the 200th anniversary of the first hot-air balloon flight, engineered by the Montgolfier brothers in France.

MONDAY
June 6

In New York, 138 people have been arrested at a sit-in at the Shoreham nuclear power plant.

TUESDAY
June 7

Michael Mackay and Ron Kistler win the billboard-sitting contest after 261 days of sitting together on top of a billboard.

WEDNESDAY
June 8

SPELLING BEE HERO: 13-year-old Andrew Flosdorf of Fonda, New York, disqualifies himself from the National Spelling Bee Championship when the judges fail to catch his misspelling of a word. "The first rule of scouting is honesty," the boy says.

ECLIPSES OF 1983

An eclipse occurs when one celestial body passes into the shadow of another. Since ancient times, eclipses have allowed scientists to study the interactions of the earth, moon, and sun. There are usually several eclipses—of the sun or the moon—visible each year somewhere in the world. Total solar eclipses are important to scientists because only then can they see and study the solar corona (the outermost atmosphere of the sun).

There are four eclipses in 1983; only the second, a partial eclipse of the moon, is visible from the United States.

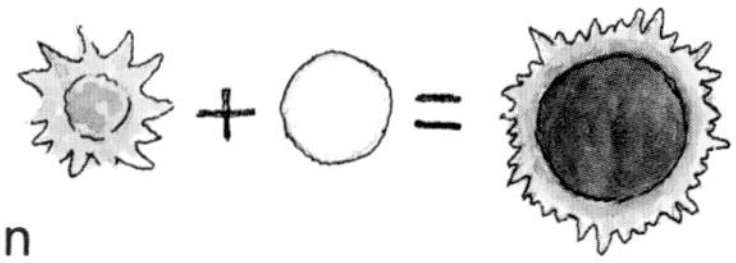

June 11: Total eclipse of the sun
June 25: Partial eclipse of the moon
December 5: Annular eclipse of the sun
December 19–20: Penumbral eclipse of the moon

In an annular eclipse of the sun, the moon covers all but a bright ring around the sun's circumference. A penumbral eclipse is one in which there is a partial shadow between the part of the moon that is eclipsed and the part that is not.

THURSDAY *June 9* — After competing with 136 other finalists, Blake Giddens becomes the 59th National Spelling Bee champion today. Winning word: Purim.

FRIDAY *June 10* — Another earthquake shakes Coalinga, California, at 8:10 P.M. • Third day of the annual Chicken Show in Wayne, Nebraska.

SATURDAY *June 11* — Total eclipse of the sun visible in Java, southern Celebes, and southern New Guinea. • In China, Zhu Jianhua sets a new world record for the high jump: 7 feet, 9½ inches.

WHO ELSE WAS BORN IN JUNE?
MAURICE SENDAK

Author and illustrator of children's books
He received the 1964 Caldecott Medal for *Where the Wild Things Are* and the 1971 Caldecott Honor for *In the Night Kitchen.*
BORN June 10, 1928, in New York City

SUNDAY
June 12

Engineers begin plugging up a 200-foot-wide sinkhole with tons of dirt in Alachua, Florida. • Beaches in southern California have been turned red by millions of tiny red crabs that have mysteriously washed ashore.

MONDAY
June 13

Pioneer 10 crosses the orbit of Neptune, the outermost planet at present, and becomes the first spacecraft ever to leave the Solar System.

TUESDAY
June 14

National Flag Day. A seven-ton flag is unfurled across two acres near the White House. • Tickets to the 1984 Olympics go on sale.

WEDNESDAY
June 15

A school janitor in Iowa has invented a special device for removing chewing gum from floors, walls, and furniture.

THURSDAY
June 16

A federal commission declares that the U.S. government should give $20,000 by way of an apology to each Japanese-American put into an American detention camp during World War II.

FRIDAY
June 17

Bathtub races in Bath, Michigan. • At Vandenberg Air Force Base in California, the MX missile completes a successful first test flight.

SATURDAY
June 18

Sally Ride, Mission Specialist, becomes the first U.S. woman in space when the shuttle *Challenger* is launched. Also on board: 150 carpenter ants and their queen, Norma!

SUNDAY
June 19

Father's Day • Carl Lewis becomes the first athlete in 97 years to win three titles in the National Outdoor Track and Field Championships in Indianapolis, Indiana.

MONDAY
June 20

Nine million dollars worth of uncut diamonds and jewelry is stolen from a jewelry store in London. • Beginning of the Watermelon Fesival in Hampton County, South Carolina, and the beginning of National Fink Week in Texas!

TUESDAY
June 21

Summer solstice. Today is the longest day (one with the most daylight) of the year. The solstice occurs at 6:09 P.M. (EST).

BALLOON HISTORY OR BALLOON RUMOR?

Many people believe the inventor of the balloon was Cyrano de Bergerac, a French soldier and poet who was famous for his long nose.

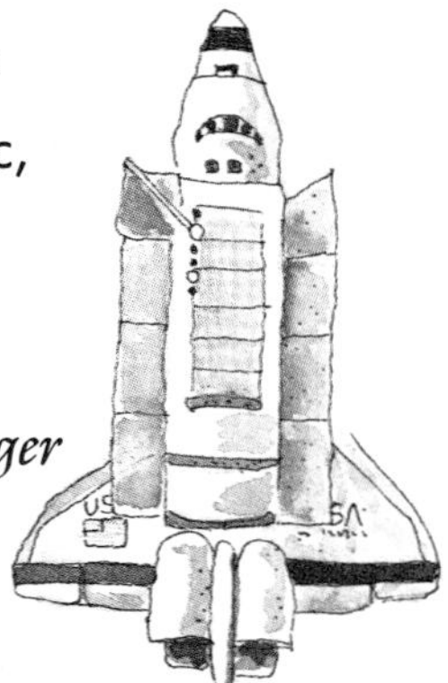

WEDNESDAY
June 22

HI-TECH SHOW-OFF: Space shuttle *Challenger* practices using its robot arm by releasing a satellite into space and then deftly recapturing it.

THURSDAY
June 23

Food and beverage makers have announced the invention of the "paper bottle," a new kind of package that is expected to replace cans and bottles.

FRIDAY
June 24

Challenger lands after 6 days and 98 orbits around the earth. • Four baby eaglets from Nova Scotia are taken to Bear Swamp, New Jersey, where they will be monitored by television cameras and tiny radio transmitters.

SATURDAY
June 25
Full Moon

Anniversary of Custer's last stand at the Battle of the Little Big Horn, 1876 • John Y. Brown, Jr., the governor of Kentucky, has open-heart surgery.

FUN FACT '83

Ants have five noses.

SMART STARLINGS?

In 1978, bird-watchers counted about 52,000 starlings roosting beneath the Connecticut Turnpike bridge over the Miamus River. In 1979, there were only 12,000. By 1980, starling searchers reported a mere 6 birds. On June 28, 1983, when the bridge collapsed, there were — none!

Did the starlings somehow sense that their home was becoming unsafe, or were they just tired of the decor?

SUNDAY
June 26

20,000 people show up to dance at the National Square Dance Convention in Louisville, Kentucky.

MONDAY
June 27

THE WORLD'S HIGHESTS: Melting snow causes the Colorado River to reach its highest level in 66 years. A painting by Mondrian is bought by a Japanese collector for $2,156,000, the highest auction price ever paid for an abstract work of art!

TUESDAY
June 28

The Connecticut Turnpike bridge over the Miamus River collapses.

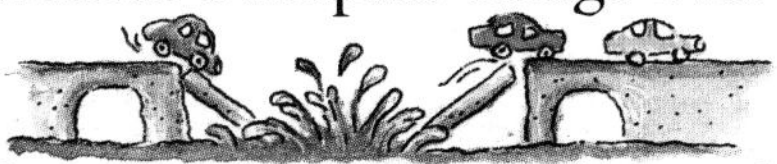

WEDNESDAY
June 29

The world's most expensive and complex communications satellite, the United States's TDRS (Tracking and Data Relay Satellite), achieves its orbit 22,236 miles above the equator—after weeks of delicate course corrections.

THURSDAY
June 30

Today is longer than any other day in 1983 by one second, which is added to make up for the gradually slowing rotation of the earth.

SALLY RIDE
FIRST U.S. WOMAN
IN SPACE

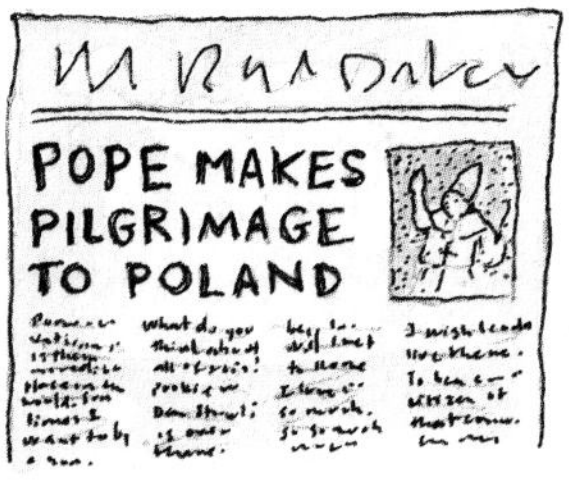
POPE MAKES
PILGRIMAGE
TO POLAND

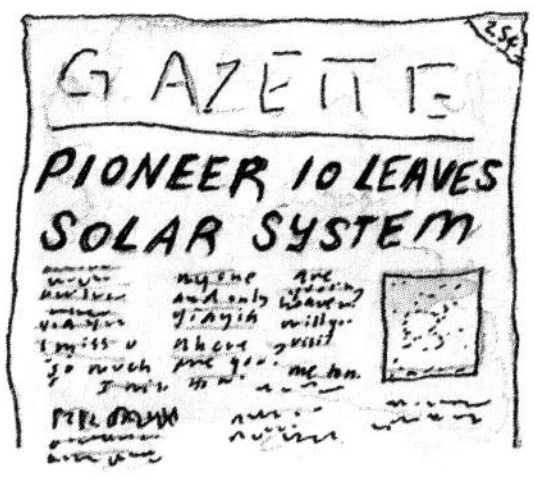
GAZETTE
PIONEER 10 LEAVES
SOLAR SYSTEM

U.S. PUBLIC HEALTH
SERVICE ANNOUNCES
AIDS NOW NUMBER
ONE PRIORITY

July

*T*his month was named to honor Julius Caesar.

BIRTHSTONE *Ruby*

FRIDAY
July 1
A reproduction of the first hot-air balloon is inflated on the Mall in Washington, D.C., part of the Air and Space Museum's celebration of 200 years of flight.

SATURDAY
July 2
Martina Navratilova wins women's singles and doubles today at the Wimbledon tennis championships. • The 10th annual cherrypit-spitting contest in Eau Claire, Michigan, is won by Rick Krause, with a distance of 53 feet, 7½ inches.

SUNDAY
July 3
John McEnroe wins the men's singles title at Wimbledon. • Mayor John Lomelo is run down by a speeding bed in Sunrise, Florida, during a fund-raising event!

MONDAY
July 4
Independence Day; also Indian Rights Day • Congratulations to Mark Schrader, the first American to sail around the world alone via the southern route!

TUESDAY
July 5
In Overland Park, Kansas, a valuable print of *Return of the Jedi* is stolen from a projectionist, who is held hostage for two hours.

WEDNESDAY
July 6

In Chicago, the Lincoln Park Zoo's 500-pound gorilla, Sinbad, has his teeth cleaned. • POPULATION EXPLOSION: Tehama County, California, reports 234 grasshoppers per square yard!

THURSDAY
July 7
Fires rage over more than 225,000 acres in six western states.

FRIDAY
July 8
11-year-old Samantha Smith from Manchester, Maine, arrives in the Soviet Union. She was invited by Soviet leader Yuri V. Andropov.

FUN FACT '83

There are more insects in one square mile of countryside than there are people in the entire world.

WHO ELSE WAS BORN IN JULY?

HENRY FORD

Automobile manufacturer
Founder and president of Ford Motor Company, he built the first inexpensive automobile, the Model T, and introduced the idea of the assembly line to industry.
BORN July 30, 1863, in Dearborn, Michigan

SATURDAY
July 9

Michael Reed, an 8-year-old who has been missing for a week on Roan Mountain in Tennessee, is found today. He survived by eating wild berries and apples.

SUNDAY
July 10

A 6-inch-long slug named Cale wins the Slug Derby in Washington State, defeating both Seattle Slug and Slug-of-War.

MONDAY
July 11

National Cheer-Up-the-Lonely Day • 20-year-old Julie Ridge swims two laps around Manhattan. She is the first person to accomplish this daring feat!

TUESDAY
July 12

A five-legged toad is found in Noble, Oklahoma.

WALLWALKER WATCH

Ken Hakuta has sold more than 15,000,000 Wacky Wallwalkers, small plastic spider-octopuses that stick to the wall when you throw them and then crawl down the wall by themselves!

WEDNESDAY
July 13

Andy, a polar bear who lives at the Atlanta Zoo, has been given his own ice machine to help him deal with the summer heat.

THURSDAY
July 14

It is 111 degrees Fahrenheit in Phoenix, Arizona. The Phoenix indoor soccer team announces it is changing its nickname from "Inferno" to something cooler.

FRIDAY
July 15

Robert Sweetgall finishes his long-distance run of 10,608 miles around the U.S., which he began in October 1982. The run started and ended in Washington, D.C.

SATURDAY
July 16
Erno Rubik, the inventor of Rubik's Cube, has been granted a patent for a new toy: Rubik's Snake.

SUNDAY
July 17
The 14th annual convention of the Jim Smith Society is held this weekend in Kings Island, Ohio. About 1,200 people named Jim Smith are attending.

MONDAY
July 18
Kids from all over the country have donated more than $188,500 for the restoration of the Statue of Liberty.

TUESDAY
July 19
For the second time in 48 hours, a plane is hijacked to Cuba. It's the ninth hijacking to Cuba so far this year.

WEDNESDAY
July 20
Anniversary of man's first landing on the moon in 1969 • Hog-calling contest is held in Baltimore, Maryland.

WHAT'S HOT

Cabbage Patch dolls
Animal slippers
Return of the Jedi lunch boxes
Wacky Wallwalkers
BMX bikes
Trivial Pursuit
Dungeons and Dragons
Ripped clothing (thanks to the movie *Flashdance*)
Michael Jackson
Care Bears
The Marilyn Monroe doll

THURSDAY
July 21
It's minus 128.6 degrees Fahrenheit at Vostok in Antarctica, the lowest temperature ever recorded! • In Minneapolis, Minnesota, a tap-dancing record is set (4.1 miles) by a group of 22 tap dancers.

FRIDAY
July 22
In New Mexico, a giant balloon is tested that may one day be used to drop a spacecraft on Jupiter.

SATURDAY
July 23
LOON COUNTING: 700 volunteers check Maine's lakes for loons to see how the bird is surviving in the environment.

SUNDAY
July 24

Full Moon
The U.S. Fish and Wildlife Service in South Carolina is searching for people to help count alligators.

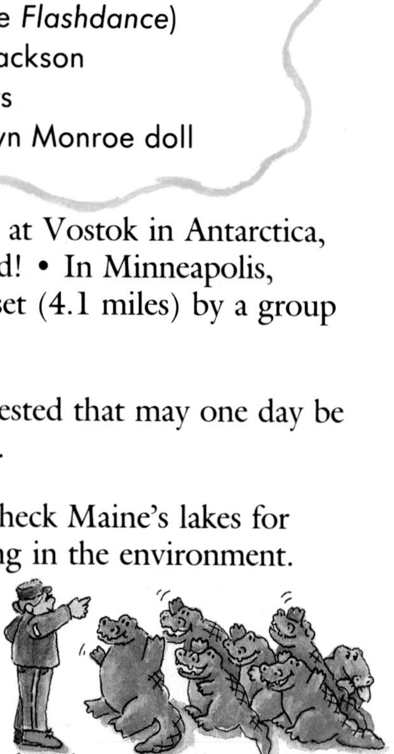

MONDAY
July 25
Jessie Alma Edge, 83, is sworn into the city council today in Niceville, Florida. She is the oldest first-time elected official in the country.

TUESDAY
July 26

U.S. athlete Mary Slaney runs 1,500 meters in 3 minutes, 57.12 seconds, setting a world record.

WEDNESDAY
July 27

Second annual International Worm Race in Johnson City, Tennessee. The race is run on mud-covered cardboard in order to avoid the heat-related worm deaths of the year before.

THURSDAY
July 28

50th anniversary of the first singing telegram • An Amtrak train collides with a truck near Wilmington, Delaware.

FRIDAY
July 29

In New York City's Central Park, Michael Forester of Wheaton, Maryland, wins the 2nd annual Boomerang Tournament.

SATURDAY
July 30

National Governors' Conference in Portland, Maine • In Pelican Rapids, Minnesota, more than 11,000 leeches have been stolen from a bait shop.

SUNDAY
July 31

Police in Manhattan, responding to a call reporting a capsized boat, find instead a dead 40-foot-long whale floating in the Hudson River.

HAPPY BIRTHDAY, SINGING TELEGRAM...

A telegram is a message sent electrically through wire and then usually hand-delivered. The Singing Telegram, a telegram that could actually be sung to the recipient instead of just delivered, was introduced by Western Union on July 28, 1933. The first musical message was reportedly sung to Rudy Vallee (a famous singer) at the Astor Hotel in New York City on his birthday. The new service became very popular with customers. After 1950, however, all the singing was done by telephone.

FIRE RAGES IN SIX WESTERN STATES

700 SEARCH FOR LOONS IN MAINE

August

*A*ugust was named in honor of Roman emperor Augustus, whose lucky month it was.

BIRTHSTONE *Peridot*

MONDAY *August 1* — Today it becomes a law in Minnesota to be a Good Samaritan. Anyone who fails to help another person in an emergency can be fined.

TUESDAY *August 2* — The National Center for Atmospheric Research announces that it is launching a $3.5 million program to study the effects of acid rain in the U.S.

WEDNESDAY *August 3* — Twenty-year-old Anne Marie Pike of Cyprus, California, breaks two women's world records in the Ladies Professional Bowlers Tournament Classic, with scores of 1,943 for eight games and 1,142 for four games.

THURSDAY *August 4* — New York Yankee Dave Winfield is arrested for cruelty to animals after accidentally killing a seagull with a baseball in Toronto, Canada.

FRIDAY *August 5* — JAWS! A great white shark measuring 15½ feet and weighing over 2,800 pounds is caught in Long Island Sound.

SATURDAY *August 6* — The Munchkins of the International Wizard of Oz Club meet in Chester, Pennsylvania. • 65 hot-air balloons compete in the Northeast Regional Balloon Championships in Bloomsbury, New Jersey.

SUNDAY *August 7* — Family Day • In Hollywood, California, a screening of one of the longest movies ever made, the West German *Berlin Alexanderplatz*, is just letting out after 15 hours, 21 minutes!

MONDAY *August 8* — The New Jersey State Supreme Court rules that a high school locker cannot be freely searched, describing it as a student's "home away from home."

TUESDAY
August 9

WHIPPED CREAM CAPER: A man wearing a diaper enters a store in Maryland and proceeds to spray it with whipped cream —through a hose!

WEDNESDAY
August 10

In Rock Springs, Wyoming, authorities have discovered that the beavers building dams in Currant Creek are actually helping to stop erosion.

THURSDAY
August 11

Topps Chewing Gum Company and the Amurol Products Company launch the same new product: soft bubble gum in a tube. Amurol is calling theirs Tubble gum.

FRIDAY
August 12

The FBI has discovered that a group of Wisconsin teenagers with home computers are guilty of tampering with approximately 60 high-security computer systems in the U.S. and Canada.

Meteor showers!

THE CENTURY'S HOTTEST AUGUST

The year 1983 was one of extreme weather in the U.S. On September 20, the National Weather Service declared August 1983 to be the hottest August on record. Although complete national records go back only as far as 1931, many local records showed it to be the hottest August in 100 years!

SATURDAY
August 13

About 8,000 people in Caldwell, Idaho, celebrate the town's 100th birthday by eating a ton of hash-brown potatoes and a sixty-foot-long link sausage!

SUNDAY
August 14

Special U.S. space stamps with a $9.35 denomination—higher than that of any previous stamp—are issued for letters which will orbit earth on board the next space-shuttle flight.

MONDAY
August 15

Two Seattle-area fishermen will split $1 million in prize money for catching specially marked salmon in a fishing derby in Puget Sound.

TUESDAY
August 16

The U.S. Department of Energy sets up a study for a new superconductivity collider, a huge machine for smashing atoms.

WEDNESDAY
August 17

Happy birthday to Davy Crockett, who was born on this day in 1786! • An earthquake strikes Luzon, the largest island in the Philippines.

THURSDAY
August 18

Hurricane Alicia strikes Houston, Texas, with winds of 115 miles an hour. • In Spring, Texas, two armadillos get married!

FRIDAY
August 19

National Aviation Day • An 80-foot-long hot-air balloon is inflated at the American Museum of Natural History in New York City.

SATURDAY
August 20

The queen of Swaziland is ousted, and it is announced that the new king will be Makhosetive, a schoolboy.

SUNDAY
August 21

The temperature reaches a record-breaking 110 degrees Fahrenheit in North Carolina.

MONDAY
August 22

One of the 22 copies of the Declaration of Independence printed in Philadelphia, Pennsylvania, in 1776 is sold to Williams College in Williamstown, Massachusetts, for $412,500.

FUN FACT '83

Your hair and your fingernails grow faster in the summer.

TUESDAY
August 23
Full Moon

A panda named Xingyue (which means "star and moon") is born at the Shanghai Zoo in China and will be given round-the-clock care at a children's hospital.

WEDNESDAY
August 24

Earthquake shakes northwest California.

THURSDAY
August 25

Two children flying a kite stop the air traffic at the Hancock County Airport in Maine for about a half-hour. One plane just misses hitting the kite at 700 feet!

FRIDAY
August 26

Women's Equality Day • The state fairs in Alaska and Oregon both begin today.

SATURDAY
August 27

At least 250,000 people participate in a March for Jobs, Peace, and Freedom in Washington, D.C., to commemorate the 20th anniversary of Martin Luther King, Jr.'s famous March on Washington in 1963.

SUNDAY
August 28

A diver in Los Angeles Harbor begins inflating 4,000 plastic trash bags, which he has stapled to a sunken 120-foot-long schooner, hoping to refloat and restore it.

WHO ELSE WAS BORN IN AUGUST?

MICHAEL JACKSON

Singer and superstar
The "Peter Pan of Pop" was originally from the group The Jackson Five. In 1983, he won two Grammy awards, for his hit single "Beat It" and for his album *Thriller*, which, by the end of 1983, sold more than 20,000,000 copies worldwide.
BORN August 29, 1958, in Gary, Indiana

MONDAY
August 29
A 70-year-old man recovers his life savings, a $100,000 bond, after having accidentally left it in a copy machine.

TUESDAY
August 30
The U.S. space shuttle *Challenger* is launched today with the country's first black astronaut, Guion S. Bluford, Jr., on board. The shuttle is also carrying the first space letters.

WEDNESDAY
August 31
The U.S.'s Edwin Corley Moses sets a world record for hurdling 400-meters—on his own 28th birthday!

TOP TEN SINGLES OF 1983*

1.	"Down Under"	Men at Work
2.	"Africa"	Toto
3.	"Baby, Come to Me"	Patti Austin with James Ingram
4.	"Billie Jean"	Michael Jackson
5.	"Come On, Eileen"	Dexys Midnight Runners
6.	"Beat It"	Michael Jackson
7.	"Let's Dance"	David Bowie
8.	"Flashdance"	Irene Cara
9.	"Every Breath You Take"	The Police
10.	"Sweet Dreams (Are Made of This)"	Eurythmics

*Source: *Billboard.*

BLIND MAN SAILS ACROSS THE PACIFIC SOLO

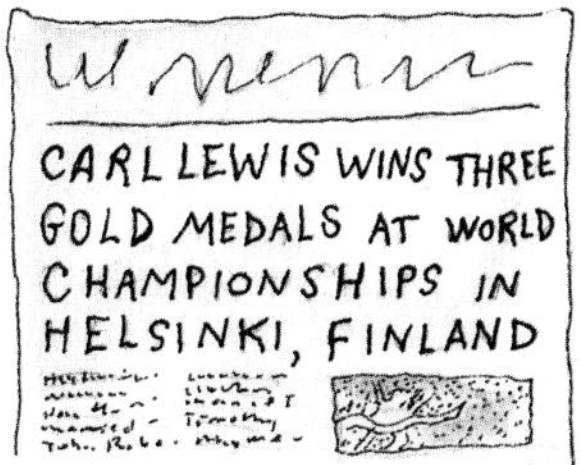
CARL LEWIS WINS THREE GOLD MEDALS AT WORLD CHAMPIONSHIPS IN HELSINKI, FINLAND

MILWAUKEE YOUTH RAIDS COMPUTERS

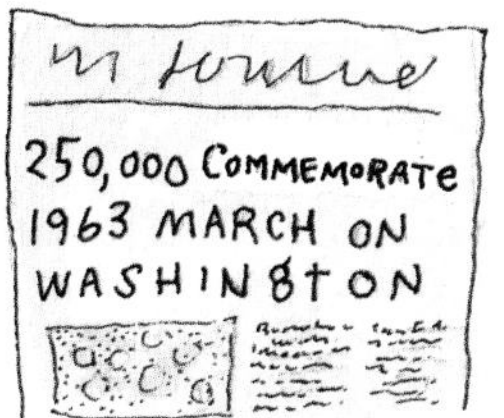
250,000 COMMEMORATE 1963 MARCH ON WASHINGTON

September

*T*he name September comes from the latin *septem*, meaning "seven." This was the seventh month of the old Roman calendar.

BIRTHSTONE *Sapphire*

THURSDAY
September 1

More than 60,000 students stay home today on an extended summer vacation, as Michigan and Illinois teachers strike.

FRIDAY
September 2

OOPS: A man in Pittsburgh, Pennsylvania, steals $1,500 from a bank by handing a note to the teller. Unfortunately for the thief, he had written the note on the back of an envelope—one with his address on the other side!

SATURDAY
September 3

Severe drought in 57 Indiana counties. • The New York Aquarium in New York City now has on display a venomous green-lace scorpion fish, *Rhinopias alphanes*, the first ever in the Americas.

SUNDAY
September 4

In Rieti, Italy, Steve Ovett of the U.S. establishes a new world record in track and field by running the 1,500-meter race in 3 minutes, 30.77 seconds.

MONDAY
September 5

Labor Day. It is also Be-Late-for-Something Day. • The space shuttle *Challenger* lands with a perfect touchdown at 12:40 A.M. PST at Edwards Air Force Base in California.

TUESDAY
September 6

According to officials, Lake Wallenpaupack in the Pocono Mountains, which was proclaimed dying a few years ago, is in surprisingly good shape this year.

WEDNESDAY
September 7

Greece and the U.S. sign a five-year defense and economic cooperation agreement in Athens. • President Reagan wears his hearing aid in public for the first time.

THURSDAY
September 8

First day of Rosh Hashanah • A former member of the Czechoslovakian cycling team escapes by dark with his wife and two children to Austria, in a makeshift balloon sewn out of raincoats.

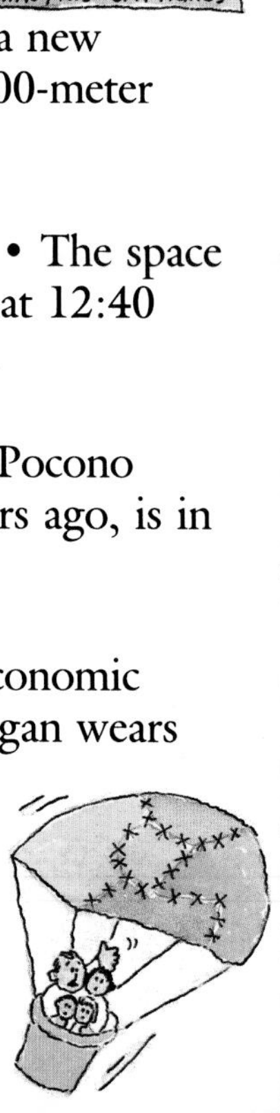

FRIDAY
September 9

Police in Huntington Beach, California, have reported two strange, possibly related robberies: $700 worth of quarters from a bank and a Pac-Man machine from a video arcade a few blocks away.

SATURDAY
September 10

HEAT WAVE CONTINUES: Temperatures in the nineties are reported from Arkansas to Michigan. • Martina Navratilova beats Chris Evert Lloyd in women's singles tennis at the U.S. Open.

SUNDAY
September 11

Grandparents' Day • Water officials in south Florida have agreed to attempt to restore the Kissimmee River to its original—clean—condition.

MONDAY
September 12

Two paintings by Picasso worth $1 million, which are on loan at the Art Museum of South Texas, are stolen.

TUESDAY
September 13

A thick fog rolls into San Francisco, providing long-awaited relief from the record heat of the last few days.

WEDNESDAY
September 14

The U.S. Postal Service issues a stamp commemorating the Metropolitan Opera, which will be 100 years old this year.

THURSDAY
September 15

In a peace gesture, an Indian swami carrying purple flowers flies over the Berlin Wall to East Germany in a motorized kite. • In Jackson, Minnesota, the first earth-covered motel, the Earth Inn, opens.

FRIDAY
September 16

An exhibition of 100 drawings from the archives of the Frank Lloyd Wright Foundation opens today in Scottsdale, Arizona.

FUN FACT '83

The British drink a great deal of tea. The average citizen sips 1,650 cups each year.

SATURDAY
September 17

Yom Kippur; also Citizenship Day • Arnold Schwarzenegger, actor and bodybuilder, becomes a citizen of the United States.

SUNDAY
September 18

The U.S. Secretary of Transportation has announced that Alaska, which stretches across four time zones, will change to one time zone starting October 30.

MONDAY
September 19

HOW RICH IS RICH? Top commodities trader Mark Rich is indicted for tax evasion of $48 million, the biggest sum in U.S. history. • Hallmark agrees to stop making posters that show Snoopy as someone who likes partying more than studying.

TUESDAY
September 20

Sixteen-year-old Eric DeWilde of Hollywood, Florida, becomes the legal owner of $1 million in jewels he found lying by the Seaboard Coast Railroad tracks on March 16.

WEDNESDAY
September 21

The temperature drops below freezing in 38 cities. • NASA assigns two female astronauts, both physicians, to space-shuttle missions in 1984.

THURSDAY
September 22
Harvest Moon

Hobbit Day • Happy birthday, ice-cream cone. Italo Marchiony applied for the patent on this date in 1903

WHAT IS A "HARVEST MOON"?

The harvest moon is the full moon nearest the time of the autumn equinox. It ushers in a period of several days when the moon rises soon after sunset. The harvest moon gives farmers extra hours of light in which to harvest their crops before frost—and winter—comes. The next full moon after harvest moon is called the hunter's moon.

FRIDAY
September 23

Autumn equinox • The workers at the Weirton Steel Works in West Virginia decide to buy the plant from National Steel Corporation, which wanted to close it down.

SATURDAY
September 24

Torrential rains in Arizona cause widespread flooding. • A mathematics professor in Fargo, North Dakota, has left his entire estate of $90,000 to provide food for local birds and squirrels.

SUNDAY
September 25

State officials and concerned citizens discuss banning moose hunting, in light of the 739 moose killed in the recent six-day moose-hunting season in Maine.

WHO ELSE WAS BORN IN SEPTEMBER?

ELIZABETH I

Queen of England
The period during which she ruled, from 1558 to 1603, later became known as the Elizabethan period.
BORN September 7, 1533, at Greenwich Palace near London, England

MONDAY
September 26
YACHT RACING: Australia wins the America's Cup, ending a 132-year U.S. reign. • Happy birthday, Johnny Appleseed, who was born on this day in 1774!

TUESDAY
September 27
Ancestor Appreciation Day; also the anniversary of the birth of Samuel Adams in 1722.

WEDNESDAY
September 28
Happy birthday, Confucius. • Publisher Farrar, Straus & Giroux announces plans to issue a 167-year-old previously unpublished Grimm's fairy tale, *Dear Mili*, to be illustrated by Maurice Sendak.

THURSDAY
September 29

With its 3,389th performance, *A Chorus Line* today becomes the longest-running Broadway show in history, an event celebrated by a special chorus line of more than 300 dancers.

FRIDAY
September 30
A new device for animals (a type of bite valve) has been invented that will allow pigs, sheep, dogs, and monkeys to get their own water.

KOREAN COMMERCIAL AIRLINER SHOT DOWN OVER SOVIET UNION
AUSTRALIA WINS AMERICA'S CUP
VANESSA WILLIAMS FIRST BLACK TO WIN MISS AMERICA

October

*O*ctober was the eighth month of the old Roman calendar; the name is from the Latin *octo*, meaning "eight."

BIRTHSTONE *Opal*

SATURDAY
October 1
Hundreds of hot-air balloons drift in the skies above Albuquerque, New Mexico, at the opening of the International Hot-Air Balloon Festival.

SUNDAY
October 2
The Chocolate Extraordinaire Festival is held in New York City, featuring chocolate in the shape of flowers, leaves, porcupines, butterflies, birds, and even houses.

MONDAY
October 3
MOTH STOWAWAYS? Beginning today, the Agriculture Department is posting officials along highways leading away from the Northeast to make sure any outdoor goods—camping equipment, building materials, yard and garden items—in transit are free of gypsy moths.

TUESDAY
October 4
The 100th anniversary of the first run of the Orient Express • In the Black Rock Desert in Nevada, Richard Noble sets a speed record of 633.468 miles per hour in his 17,000-pound thrust, Rolls Royce 302 jet-powered Thrust 2.

WEDNESDAY
October 5
Lech Walesa, the founder of Solidarity (the federation of Polish trade unions), is named recipient of the Nobel Peace Prize.

THURSDAY
October 6
Universal Children's Day • A two-month-old calf named Johnny receives an artificial heart called the Utah-100.

FRIDAY
October 7
Chairs, handmade by former President Jimmy Carter, are auctioned to benefit the Carter Presidential Library. Each chair is signed by President Carter.

SATURDAY
October 8
Today is the Madison County Covered Bridge Festival in Iowa. • An earthquake hits New York State and the surrounding areas.

SUNDAY
October 9

National Fire Prevention Week; also the anniversary of the famous Chicago fire of 1871 • A fire rages in downtown Boston!

MONDAY
October 10

Columbus Day • Soviet space probes, launched four months ago, have reached Venus and are now in orbit around the planet.

TUESDAY
October 11

Opening game of the World Series between baseball's Baltimore Orioles and the Philadelphia Phillies.

WEDNESDAY
October 12

Halley's comet, due to pass near earth in 1986, has been seen by astronomers at a distance of 1.4 billion kilometers through the world's largest telescope, which is in the Caucasus Mountains of the USSR.

THURSDAY
October 13

New computers, built to turn out artificial hips and knees, go on display in New York City.

FRIDAY
October 14

Japanese astronomers photograph two rings of dust around the sun, using a special video camera suspended by a balloon.

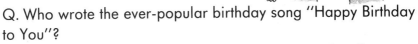

HAPPY BIRTHDAY QUIZ:

Q. Who wrote the ever-popular birthday song "Happy Birthday to You"?

A. It was composed by Mildred Hill and Patty Smith Hill, two sisters from Louisville, Kentucky, who were schoolteachers. Originally called "Good Morning to You," the song was copyrighted on October 16, 1893.

SATURDAY
October 15

In Pacific Grove, California, thousands of schoolchildren march in the 44th annual Butterfly Parade to celebrate the seasonal return of the town's monarch butterflies.

SUNDAY
October 16

The Baltimore Orioles win the World Series, four games to one, defeating the Philadelphia Phillies.

MONDAY
October 17

Bill Dunlop leaves from Miami on a trip around the world, which he is taking alone in an eight-foot sailboat.

WHO ELSE WAS BORN IN OCTOBER?

SARAH BERNHARDT

French actress
Known as "the Divine Sarah," she was famous for playing tragic and heroic roles. She continued her stage career even after her leg was amputated in 1915.
BORN October 22, 1844, in Paris, France

TUESDAY
October 18
Alaska Day • Cleveland, Ohio, holds the world's largest rummage sale.

WEDNESDAY
October 19
The Senate passes a bill making Martin Luther King, Jr.'s birthday an annual federal holiday, starting in 1986.

THURSDAY
October 20
The International Bureau of Weights and Measures today changes the way length is measured throughout the world. The new method is based on the speed of light.

FRIDAY
October 21
Hunter's Moon 
Three Americans have become the first non-Chinese to successfully climb the Tibetan side of Mt. Everest, the highest mountain in the world.

SATURDAY
October 22
Happy birthday! The New York Metropolitan Opera is 100-years-old today. 8 hours of festivities are offered by the Met.

SUNDAY
October 23
The New York City Marathon is won by Rod Dixon, of New Zealand. Time: 2 hours, 8 minutes, 59 seconds. The first woman to finish is Grete Waitz, of Norway, with a time of 2 hours, 27 minutes.

MONDAY
October 24
More than 1,200 people, including the famous child expert Dr. Benjamin Spock, are arrested during nationwide demonstrations against nuclear weapons in Europe.

FUN FACT '83

The American Chemical Society reports that the number of chemicals recorded to date has reached 6 million!

TUESDAY
October 25

U.S. invades Grenada, a small country in the Caribbean.

WEDNESDAY
October 26

A half-built Miami Beach palace belonging to Sheik Mohammed al-Fassi is auctioned today for $2.3 million. The mansion was to contain a bowling alley, a mosque, a discotheque, a bomb shelter, a guardhouse, two swimming pools, and five waterfalls!

THURSDAY
October 27

RESCUED: The Coast Guard picks up a lone survivor from a 130-foot tugboat that capsized early today in heavy seas in the Gulf of Alaska.

OCTOBER IS NATIONAL POPCORN MONTH

Popcorn is a special variety of corn called *Zea mays everta*, which has hard kernels that burst to form white, irregularly shaped puffs when heated. In the U.S., the average person eats 42 popped quarts a year! 1983's favorite popcorn flavors: piña colada, grape, and strawberry

FRIDAY
October 28

Major earthquake rocks eight northwestern states. • Twin gorillas have been born at the Columbus Zoo in Ohio!

SATURDAY
October 29

Stock market prices crashed on this day in 1929. • Secret Service agents in Los Angeles seize $5 million of fake money and three suspects in one of the nation's largest counterfeiting cases.

SUNDAY
October 30

An earthquake devastates 147 villages in Turkey. • In St. Louis, Missouri, a man climbs a thirty-story building, unrolls an American flag, and then rappels to the ground.

MONDAY
October 31

Halloween; it is also National Magic Day

ORIOLES WIN WORLD SERIES
U.S. INVADES GRENADA

November

*N*ovember was the ninth month of the old Roman calendar. The name comes from the Latin *novem*, meaning “nine.”

BIRTHSTONE *Topaz*

TUESDAY
November 1
New research shows that Japanese students are better in math than U.S. students. • IBM introduces its new personal computer, the Peanut.

WEDNESDAY
November 2
The U.S. equestrian team wins the Nation’s Cup at the 100th National Horse Show, at Madison Square Garden, New York City.

THURSDAY
November 3
In Boston, FBI agents arrest an East German physicist on spying charges.

FRIDAY
November 4
Trailways Bus Company is accommodating three times more passengers than usual because of the Greyhound strike.

SATURDAY
November 5
Leslie Burr, despite a broken collarbone, becomes Rider of the Year at the National Horse Show after winning the $25,000 Grand Prix for Open Jumpers. The horse she is riding, Albany, is named Horse of the Year.

SUNDAY
November 6
A goose smashes through the windshield of a Republic Airlines plane, injuring the pilot. The copilot lands the plane safely at the Sioux Falls airport in South Dakota.

MONDAY
November 7
Unicorn sightings are being investigated. The mythical animal has been seen by several people over the weekend at Shenandoah National Park in Virginia.

TUESDAY
November 8
Election Day • In Kentucky, Martha Collins becomes the first female governor in the state’s history and the only woman among the nation’s 50 state governors.

WEDNESDAY
November 9
A Continental Airlines jet lands on a taxiway instead of a runway in Denver, a mistake a spokesperson blames on glare from snow. The plane was carrying the president of the airline.

WHO ELSE WAS BORN IN NOVEMBER?

DANIEL BOONE

Pioneer and explorer
Boone is best known for his part in the expansion and development of lands west of the Allegheny Mountains. In 1775, he built a fort in what is now Kentucky and called it Boonesboro.
BORN November 2, 1734, in Reading, Pennsylvania

THURSDAY
November 10
"Marvelous" Marvin Hagler beats Roberto Duran in Las Vegas, retaining the Middleweight Boxing Championship title. • Violent rainstorms wreak havoc on the Pacific Coast.

FRIDAY
November 11
Veteran's Day • In the Gulf of Mexico, the cook of an oil-rig crew boat that had capsized is found alive—huddled in an air pocket! • Ed Asner is reelected as president of the Screen Actors Guild.

1983 WORST FOODS CORNER*

43% of Americans said they wouldn't eat snails
41% of Americans wouldn't eat brains
34% of Americans wouldn't eat squid
34% of Americans wouldn't eat shark
32% of Americans wouldn't eat tripe

*Source: A 1983 Gallup survey.

No way, man!

Hey, I'd eat 'em!
Heh, heh heh!

SATURDAY
November 12
Cabbage Patch dolls are introduced to the world. Each is unique and comes with its own birth certificate and certificate of adoption.

SUNDAY
November 13
At Firebird Lake in Arizona, Eddie Hill sets a speedboat record, traveling 440 yards in 5.6 seconds.

MONDAY
November 14
Thirty-six nursing-home residents, between 60 and 80 years old, are sworn in as the U.S.'s oldest Girl Scouts, Troop 2020. The troop also has thirteen men—the first adult male Girl Scouts in history.

TUESDAY
November 15
The strongest earthquake in the area since 1975 hits Hawaii at 6:13 A.M. • An oil painting, Edouard Manet's *Promenade*, sells for $3,960,000, a record for a Manet painting at auction.

WEDNESDAY
November 16

Yale University announces that their 12th bulldog mascot, "the female Handsome Dan," will be retiring at age ten, after the 100th football game between Yale and Harvard.

THURSDAY
November 17

At the White House Symposium on Physical Fitness and Sports, "plyometrics"—hopping, bounding, and jumping off boxes—is predicted to be the next exercise craze.

FRIDAY
November 18

Scientists have new evidence that antibiotics may actually be effective against up to one-third of all sore throats.

SATURDAY
November 19

In Bloomington, Indiana, Purdue University students battle Indiana University students in an ice-cream-eating contest.

SUNDAY
November 20
Full Moon

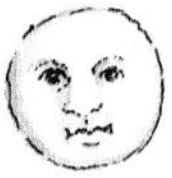

The National Council of Teachers debates the use of computers in elementary and high schools. • 25,000 pounds of dynamite explodes in an unmarked storage bunker in Des Moines, Iowa, leaving a 72- by 30-foot crater.

MONDAY
November 21

Baltimore, Maryland, opens its $797 million subway, almost seventeen years after the planning began.

TUESDAY
November 22

The world's largest solar-power plant to date starts up in Carrizo Plain, California. By 1985, it is expected to produce energy for 6,400 homes.

THANKSGIVING TIDBIT

Thanksgiving has been a national holiday in the U.S. since 1789. It commemorates the first harvest reaped by the colonists of Plymouth, Massachusetts. In 1983, the average American's Thanksgiving dinner has 1,500 calories, about twice the amount in an average meal.

WEDNESDAY
November 23

Two Soviet cosmonauts return to earth after spending 150 days in the *Salyut-7* space station.

THURSDAY
November 24

Thanksgiving • Two million people watch Macy's Thanksgiving Day Parade in New York City. • In Chicago, a Florida-bound jet is forced to turn around and land after a sea gull is sucked into one of its engines.

FRIDAY
November 25

Seven unclaimed sheep found wandering the streets of Springfield, Missouri, are auctioned off today.

PET NAMES

The most popular names for dogs and cats in 1983*

Dogs	Cats
1. Pepper	1. Sam/Samantha
2. Brandy	2. Kitty
3. Lady	3. Tiger
4. Bear	4. Boots
5. Rocky	5. Patches

*Source: Anderson Animal Shelter in South Elgin, Illinois.

SATURDAY
November 26 In London, $40 million worth of gold is stolen near Heathrow Airport. It is the largest theft in British history.

SUNDAY
November 27 THE CABBAGE CRAZE: More than 25,000 people nationwide line up outside Zayre Corporation's 275 stores to buy Cabbage Patch dolls. In less than a half-hour, 60,000 dolls are sold.

FUN FACT '83

The average person loses more hair in November than in any other month.

NOVEMBER

MONDAY
November 28 A record November blizzard (including 19 inches of snow in Kansas) brings middle western cities to a standstill. • The space shuttle *Columbia* carries *Spacelab*, a European-built research station, into orbit.

TUESDAY
November 29 A 45-ton female right whale has been seen with a calf off the Massachusetts coast, giving scientists new hope for the future of this rare breed.

WEDNESDAY
November 30 Michael Jackson announces he will team up with his brothers once again for a world concert tour.

MICHAEL JACKSON
ANNOUNCES WORLD TOUR
$40 MILLION IN GOLD
STOLEN IN LONDON
25¢
CABBAGE PATCH
DOLLS CAUSE PANIC

December

*D*ecember used to be the tenth month of the year (the Latin *decem* means "ten"). The old Roman calendar began with March.

BIRTHSTONE *Turquoise*

THURSDAY
December 1

Hanukkah begins at sunset. • Rice farmers across the U.S are now raising crayfish in their rice paddies. The sales of the crayfish will help make up for the low price of rice.

FRIDAY
December 2

LOVE AT FIRST FLIGHT: Two trapeze artists are wed in Venice, Florida, and are led to their wedding reception by a parade of clowns, 21 elephants, 13 tigers, 6 camels, and 2 llamas. The bride tosses her bouquet while performing a daring duet in the air with her husband.

SATURDAY
December 3

An expedition from the Woodland Institute of Spruce Knobb, West Virginia, reports that they have found evidence in Nepal of a new species of bear, which weighs about 150 pounds and nests in trees 50 feet above the ground.

SUNDAY
December 4

An annular eclipse of the sun is visible over the eastern Atlantic Ocean, southern Europe, and Africa. • In Athol, Massachusetts, eight brothers and sisters meet after being separated for fifty years.

MONDAY
December 5

Tinsel Day • At 6:06 P.M., the Rockefeller Center Christmas tree in New York City is lit by schoolchildren, who throw the switch that turns on thousands of lights on the 75-foot-tall tree.

TUESDAY
December 6

A West German group pays the largest sum ever ($11.7 million) for a work of art, the *Gospels of Henry the Lion*, an illustrated book created by a Benedictine monk in 1174.

WEDNESDAY
December 7

More than 700 specialists meet for a three-day conference on how to save the Chesapeake Bay from being destroyed by pollution.

THURSDAY
December 8

The space shuttle *Columbia*, with a six-man crew including one West German astronaut, lands at Edwards Air Force Base in California after ten days in space.

FRIDAY
December 9

People are already coming to see Mr. Rudd's Christmas decorations in Blue Creek, Ohio. Every day in December, at 5:30 P.M., he switches on 20 acres of Christmas lights, several 500-pound fiberglass angels, and 3 crosses.

SATURDAY
December 10

Human Rights Day • The Nobel Prize ceremony is held in City Hall in Oslo, Norway. Danuta Walesa accepts the Peace prize for her husband, Lech Walesa.

SUNDAY
December 11

Revelers at Buchbinder's Restaurant in New York City release a half-dozen colorful balloons into the wind. They are found the next day at Michelle Lambert's house in Nova Scotia–750 miles away!

MONDAY
December 12

HO HO HO: White House Counselor Edwin Meese dresses up as Santa Claus at a dinner party of fellow Republicans.

TUESDAY
December 13

The Detroit Pistons beat the Denver Nuggets in basketball in Denver, Colorado. Score: an amazing 186-184!

WEDNESDAY
December 14

The White House is sending out 75,000 Christmas cards.

THURSDAY
December 15

Bill of Rights Day • The space shuttle *Columbia* returns to the Kennedy Space Center in Florida.

FRIDAY
December 16

Family dogs are attacking herds of antelope that have been driven by severe snowstorms to seek shelter in neighborhoods in Rawlins, Wyoming.

1983 NOBEL PRIZE WINNERS

The famous Nobel awards are named after the inventor of dynamite, Alfred B. Nobel. The prizes are officially awarded each year on December 10.

Peace: Lech Walesa, of Poland
Physics: Subrahmanyan Chandrasekhar and William A. Fowler, both of the United States
Chemistry: Henry Taube, of Canada
Medicine: Barbara McClintock, of the United States
Literature: William Golding, of Great Britain
Economics: Gerard Debreu, of the United States

WHO ELSE WAS BORN IN DECEMBER?

LOUIS PASTEUR

French chemist and microbiologist
Known best for developing the process known as pasteurization, (used for sterilizing milk), he is also famous for his germ theory of disease, which suggested that diseases are caused by living germs.
BORN December 27, 1822, in Dole, France

SATURDAY
December 17
Wright Brothers Day. 80 years ago, the first airplane flight took place near Kitty Hawk, North Carolina.

SUNDAY
December 18
Greyhound bus drivers agree to a new three-year contract, ending a seven-week strike.

MONDAY
December 19
Twelve birds, including a scarlet macaw worth $2,500, are stolen from the Prospect Park Zoo in Brooklyn, New York.

TUESDAY
December 20
Full Moon 
Former President Gerald Ford appears on the television show *Dynasty*. • Bob Hope leaves to entertain 1,800 U.S. troops stationed in Lebanon.

FUN HOLIDAY FACTS

Last year, 28,376,389 Christmas trees were sold.

The average American eats 10.8 pounds of turkey per year, 4.3 pounds of it during the holiday season.

WEDNESDAY
December 21
North Reading, Massachusetts, is visited by mysterious airborne gooey blobs—grayish white and oily-smelling globs that vanish when they hit the ground. The local authorities are baffled.

THURSDAY
December 22
Winter solstice • Record low temperatures throughout the U.S. • The U.S. Postal Service announces that holiday mail this year will reach a record volume of more than 10 billion pieces.

FRIDAY
December 23
Larenza Mungin catches a 20-pound, 9-ounce southern flounder in Nassau Sound, Florida, the largest southern flounder ever caught!

SATURDAY
December 24

Christmas Eve • Hundreds of turkey dinners are delivered to needy families in New York City. • Giant bonfires are lit on the levee edging the Mississippi River, to light the way for the Christmas spirit.

SUNDAY
December 25

Christmas • A dozen American children offer a Christmas Day message of peace to China's prime minister, Zhao Ziyang. • A cat named Charcoal saves a family in Alabama from a Christmas-morning fire by jumping onto her sleeping owner's chest.

MONDAY
December 26

It is so cold that oranges freeze on the trees in Florida.

TUESDAY
December 27

Two more Soviet satellites are launched, *Cosmos 1516* and *Cosmos 1517*.

WEDNESDAY
December 28

Citizens of Houston, Texas, donate bamboo for Yin, the local zoo's panda whose own bamboo (her food supply) froze after 110 hours of below-freezing temperatures.

THURSDAY
December 29

For nearly 12 hours, 120 skiers are stranded in cable cars near Lugano, Switzerland, before they are rescued by helicopter.

FRIDAY
December 30

American Telephone & Telegraph, the Bell Telephone Company, prepares to break into eight separate companies, ending one of the largest monopolies in the world.

SATURDAY
December 31

New Year's Eve. As thousands of people in New York City's Times Square watch the Big Apple ball descend to bring in the new year, a lighted elevator descends in a similar ceremony in Columbus, Ohio.

25¢
GERMANY PAYS $11.5 MILLION FOR MEDIEVAL BOOK

ORANGES FREEZE ON TREES IN FLORIDA

YOUR YEAR AT A GLANCE

A lot happened the year you were born. How many events shown on the cover can you identify? Turn the page upside down for the answers.

1. Halley's Comet sighted (October 12) **2.** Astronauts walk in space (April 7) **3.** King Kong's 50th birthday (April 6) **4.** The ice cream cone was invented 80 years ago (September 22) **5.** Julius Caeser (See July) **6.** Rockefeller Center Christmas tree, New York City (December 5) **7.** Five hundred thousand starlings settle in Washington, Missouri (January 8) **8.** Shark caught in Long Island Sound (August 5) **9.** Kids donate over $188,500 to Statue of Liberty (July 18) **10.** New Jersey students release balloons (May 26) **11.** Tokyo Disneyland opens (April 15) **12.** Washington Redskins win Super Bowl (January 30) **13.** Seventh-grader wins Central Park sailboat race in New York City (May 10) **14.** Michael Jackson's *Thriller* album sells 20,000,000 copies this year (See August) **15.** Wright Brothers Day (December 17) **16.** Scuba divers hold underwater sing-along (April 10) **17.** U.S. Fish and Wildlife Service searches for alligator counters (July 24) **18.** New York Metropolitan Opera's 100th birthday (October 22) **19.** Brooklyn Bridge celebrates its centennial (May 24) **20.** Cabbage Patch dolls introduced (November 12) **21.** Ronald Reagan, President of the U.S. 1980–88 **22.** Anniversary of first hot-air balloon flight (March 31) **23.** Space shuttle *Challenger* launched (June 18 and August 30)